MW01200246

From
CHAOS
To
CONTROL

How to Standardize Processes and Create Effective Work Procedures

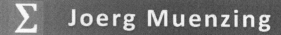

Σ Joerg Muenzing

From

Chaos

to

Control

How to Standardize
Processes and Create
Effective Work
Procedures

From

Chaos

to

Control

JOERG MUENZING

From Chaos to Control

Disclaimer

This book is presented solely for educational purposes. The author and publisher are not offering it as legal, accounting, or other professional services advice. While best efforts have been used in preparing this book, the author and publisher make no representations or warranties of any kind and assume no liabilities of any kind with respect to the accuracy or completeness of the contents and specifically disclaim any implied warranties of merchantability or fitness of use for a particular purpose. Neither the author nor the publisher shall be held liable or responsible to any person or entity with respect to any loss or incidental or consequential damages caused, or alleged to have been caused, directly or indirectly, by the information or programs contained herein. No warranty may be created or extended by sales representatives or written sales materials. Every company is different and the advice and strategies contained herein may not be suitable for your situation. You should seek the services of a competent professional before beginning any improvement program.

ISBN-10: 1466368403
ISBN-13: 978-1466368408

Cover and book design by JuggernautPress.com
First Edition

This book is dedicated to those who wish to get more predictable results with less work

Contents

INTRODUCTION

"If the staff lacks policy guidance (procedures) against which to test decisions, their
decisions will be random." - Donald Henry
Rumsfeld, 13th U.S. Secretary of Defense

*P*rocesses rule the world, and whether we
like it or not, processes control a big part
of our lives. We might even venture to say
the following: Our entire life is one big process con-
sisting of many smaller processes. This profound
statement indicates that the results we achieve
are largely dependent on the processes we follow,
that "we get what we do." The more we are aware
of these processes, the better we can steer and influence the result—and the more control we gain
over the outcome of our lives. In other words, if we
control the procedures that govern our lives, we

gain control over our destiny, and that's our starting point for this book:

Control the process to control the result.

Yes, this statement is simple, but its meaning is profound, and therefore it is a good assumption to get us started.

Keep in mind that every result depends not only on things we can influence but also on things out of our control, such as changes in the environment we operate in. This is because of the following fundamental relationship:

Result = Process + Environmental Factors

This verbal equation has several implications. First and foremost, it takes into account that external forces are always present, and these factors can and do impact the overall result. No matter how perfect our process is, environmental factors come into play. We must recognize this and account for it.

Another implication is evident when we consider the extreme situation in which no formal process exists. In this case, the equation becomes:

Result = Environmental Factors

This relationship indicates the result would depend entirely on external forces and thus the outcome would tend to be highly random. Outcomes governed by this relationship could be disastrous for most business scenarios.

In practice, businesses usually have some process associated with each task, and the process can be informal (verbal instructions) or more formal (written instructions). In any case, it is insightful to consider the extremes.

In the above equations, "Environmental Factors" refers to those things we have little or no control over, and "Process" relates to those elements we control with our formal procedures. The equal sign is not meant to be taken literally; rather, it implies there is a direct relationship between the components of the equation.

Note that this book focuses on what we *can* influence, and that is *the process* itself, not so much the environmental factors. Note also that following the steps outlined in this book will not guarantee your success, but doing so will *significantly increase* your chances of success, where "success" refers to getting what you expect.

So how do we get better control over a process and the results?

We create and implement policies and procedures that specify the best way to think, plan, and work.

Graphically, we can visualize this concept as follows:

Set Procedure > Control Process > Get Results

In the following chapters, we will discuss how to standardize work processes and create highly effective, professional procedures. This is achieved by using work standards. The exercises at the end of this book will allow you to test your understanding and apply your knowledge of these topics. Ultimately, you will create your own work standard.

The primary role of a work standard is to guide users through every step of a process, specifying exactly what to do and how to do it. Properly constructed work standards make work processes reliable and ensure predictable results. In effect, work standards are used to train people and manage their output in a consistent fashion; the decision-making and physical labor are delegated to those closest to the actual work. Thus, work standards free managers from operational tasks, allowing them to focus on strategic tasks that will *grow* the business rather than *sustain* it.

As a result, processes run faster and smoother with shorter cycles. They produce less waste and fewer mistakes, resulting in a much higher quality (sigma level). When work standards are implemented into the workflow, processes are guaranteed to become leaner while delivering more value to the customer at a lower cost to the provider.

Are you ready to get better results with less work?

OK, let's discuss the basic theory behind processes, standards, and procedures in the following chapter.

About Processes, Procedures, and Standards

"If you can't describe what you are doing as a process, you don't know what you're doing."
- William Edwards Deming, American statistician, professor, author, lecturer, and consultant, 1900 – 1993

Processes

Simply put, a process is a series of steps taken to achieve a desired result.

Technically speaking, "processing" describes the action of converting something from one state into another state through a well-established routine:

- o Groceries into a meal
- o Components into a product
- o Data into useful information

- o Reports into decisions
- o Chemicals into compounds
- o Defects into quality
- o Trainees into specialists

To illustrate, we can use the metaphor of a roadmap. If the result is the destination, then the process is the vehicle, and the procedure is the map showing the driver the best route to travel there.

Vehicle > Map > Driver > Destination

Process > Procedure > User > Result

The Process Hierarchy

Processes can be organized hierarchically, with the following three levels: (1) Mega, (2) Macro, and (3) Micro.

Strategic planning happens at the Mega level, budgeting and product development at the Macro level, and day-to-day work on the Micro level.

- o *Micro* – Short-term strategy (daily, quarterly), deals with daily operations and execution
- o *Macro* – Medium-term strategy (one to two years), products features and budgets

o *Mega* – Long-term strategy (greater than two years), markets, and investments

While this book focuses on the Micro level, providing guidance to standardize day-to-day processes, the same principles can be applied to upstream processes that exist on the Macro and Mega level. For example, budgeting, business development, company acquisitions, and business strategy would fall into these upper-level categories.

In most cases, I recommend that you start with short-term, micro processes and then expand the learning to more complex processes, such as long-term planning and business strategy. This approach will return quicker feedback and therefore shorten the learning curve.

The Process House

The "Process House" is a simplistic model used in manufacturing and services to organize processes around a value-chain. You can think of this concept as follows: core processes *build* the value-chain, while support-processes *enable* the value-chain.

Core Processes

o SCM – Supply Chain Management (sourcing and logistics)

- o PLM – Product Lifecycle Management
  (engineering, research, technology)
- o MFG – Manufacturing
  (product, operations, delivery)
- o CRM – Customer Relationship Management
  (commercial , sales, marketing, service)

Support Processes
- o HR – Human Resources (people)
- o FC – Finance and Controlling (money)
- o IT – Information Technology (reports)
- o QM – Quality Management (excellence)

Graphically, we can represent the Process House as follows:

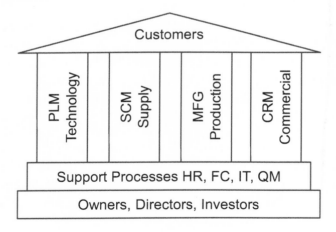

Since most companies today are organized by functions—for example Sales and Marketing, Engineering, Manufacturing, Logistics, Finance, Quality etc—the Process House model can be adapted to any business.

For example, let us consider a typical service company. For this type of business, you would need (1) a commercial process to promote and sell the service, (2) a technical process to develop service features, (3) a sourcing process to purchase hardware, software, and assistance from third parties, and (4) a service delivery process, which is equivalent to the production process in a manufacturing business.

Measuring Process Quality

When considering the quality of your current process, you might ask yourself the simple question:

How good is my process?

Processes can be assessed by either their capability (a number) or their characteristics (a level). Several methods exist, and a lot of literature is available on these topics. Rather than going into excessive detail, we will discuss two quick and simple ways to assess your process:

o Quantitative assessment – a common approach is to use the Six Sigma Model.

o Qualitative assessment – a common approach is to use the Capability Maturity Model.

Six Sigma Model

The Six Sigma model measures process variability, which is a good indicator of quality. The small Greek letter "sigma" (σ) stands for variability; in particular, how much the result deviates from the target. In this discussion, I am simplifying the model to make it easier to understand and apply.

One Sigma stands for one standard deviation. Standard deviation means "typical variation," where "typical" means when 2/3 of all results are included.

Let's illustrate with an example. Imagine that your business is responsible for filling 10,000-gallon tanks. Your customers expect 10,000 gallons but accept plus or minus 10 gallons. So the "tolerance" in this process is 10 gallons.

To evaluate how good your process is, you decide to take several samples and calculate the standard deviation. After you enter the numbers (into your Excel spreadsheet or pocket calculator), you calculate the standard deviation to be 4 gallons for example.

This means that when you fill a "typical" tank (typical in this case means 2/3 of all tanks), you fill it within 4 gallons of 10,000. The sigma level is the customer tolerance limit (10 gallons) divided by the typical variation (4 gallons), or 10/4 = 2.5 Sigma. In this case, to achieve a 6 Sigma quality level, the typical variation of the filling process must be 10 gallons divided by 6 Sigma, or 1.67 gallons.

How much sigma do I really need?

Critical processes must operate at high sigma levels (this means with low variability), while uncritical processes may allow for lower sigma levels (thus a higher variability). Airline safety for example runs at 7 Sigma, while a customer service process might provide a 3 Sigma customer satisfaction rate. As a rule of thumb, to gain an advantage in the market, your process quality should be at least 0.5 Sigma better than your closest competitor's.

How do I calculate sigma level?

Sigma level can easily be determined from defect rate or yield. Defects are measured in Defects Per Million Opportunities (DPMO). Yield is measured by the number of transactions that run perfectly the first time divided by the total number of trans-actions. For example:

Sigma level 2 yields 69%

Sigma Level	Yield	Defects DPMO*
1	31%	691,462
2	69%	308,538
3	93.3%	66,807
4	99.38%	6,210
5	99.977%	233
6	99.99966%	3.4

* - Defects per million opportunities

Example:

You place 100 orders, of which 69 are delivered on time and 31 are not. That indicates the supply process is currently functioning at a 2 Sigma quality level. In other words, for every 1 million orders placed, roughly 308,000 will be delivered late.

How many defects will your customer tolerate?

The Capability Maturity Model

To assess the current situation and set a clear im-provement target, we often use the Capability Maturity Model. This model is commonly applied in business administration, software development, and human capital management. The model defines five levels, from 'Initial' to 'Optimizing':

1. *Level 1 – Initial State* – The process is chaotic, ad hoc, reactive, undocumented, unstable, continuous fire fighting, and may involve individual heroics.

2. *Level 2 – Repeatable* – The process is documented and some parts are repeatable, but leads to inconsistent results and low discipline.

3. *Level 3 – Defined* – The process is confirmed as standard with evidence of continuous improvement.

4. *Level 4 – Managed* – The process is quantitatively managed according to agreed metrics. Process capability is established.

5. *Level 5 – Optimizing* – The process is managed with a focus on perfecting performance through improvement and innovation.

To assess your quality level, look at your key processes and ask:

o Where am I today?
o What does my customer expect?
o Where are my competitors?

o Where do I need to be next year?

To secure your future, you need to meet your customer's expectations—that's a given. But to gain a true competitive advantage, you need to perform better than your best competitor.

By following the guidelines in this book, you can gain one level each year and reach level 5 within a few years. As a result, you will discover reliable processes through standard processes as a key source of your competitiveness.

> "Quality is never an accident; it is always the result of high intention, sincere effort, intelligent direction and skillful execution; it represents the wise choice of many alternatives."
> - William A. Foster, US Marine, 1917–1945

The Hard Rules of Process Management

1. If you don't like the results, change the process to get the results you like.
2. You can't judge work if you haven't provided the standard.
3. Without a standard, decisions and results will be random.

4. Without a standard as a reference point, people are set up for failure. It's like playing soccer without rules, lines, goals, or scores.
5. If you haven't regularly upgraded processes and procedures, your competitors will eventually bypass you—it's just a matter of time.

Limitations: process management principles work well for *repetitive* work but not very well for *creative* processes. This means they will not be effective when creating paintings, music, or breakthrough innovations.

Eliminating Waste Makes a Process Lean!

All processes produce "value" and "waste." Lean Thinkers define value as something—an activity, item, or feature—a customer is willing to pay for, while everything else is considered waste.

This means that each process step adds either value (to the customer) or cost (to the provider). When standardizing processes and creating standard procedures, we must therefore carefully consider, question, evaluate, and rethink each activity:

o What are the right steps?
(Think: effectiveness, doing the right thing)
o What's the best way to do it?
(Think: efficiency, doing things right)

To improve our ability to create lean procedures, let's repeat the basics of lean and waste elimination.

Lean Basics and the 8 Wastes by "TIM WOODS"

Lean thinkers identified 8 types of waste. Reducing those wastes makes a process lean. The 8 wastes can easily be remembered as "TIM WOODS" = **T**ransport, **I**nventory, **M**otion, **W**aiting, **O**verproduction, **O**verprocessing, **D**efects, and wasted **S**kills:

- o *Transport* – unnecessary movement of people, material and information between processes
- o *Inventory* – items and information waiting to be processed or sold, such as raw materials, work in process (parts, semi-finished goods, unanswered emails, pending performance reviews, open decisions), and finished goods in stock
- o *Motion* – unnecessary movement, such as bending, stretching, reaching due to sub-optimal layout and poor ergonomics
- o *Waiting* – any time spent waiting on items, information, equipment, or people— waiting for a computer to boot or a superior to make a decision
- o *Overproduction* – making too many items or making them too early, producing ahead

of demand or in excess quantity inflates inventory and causes additional wastes from excess transportation, motion, and risk of defects

o *Overprocessing* – excessively precise, providing better quality or adding unnecessary features increases cost without adding any value to the customer

o *Defects* – doing the work more than once due to unacceptable quality—any error or failure, requiring rectification—causing rework, repair, return, or scrap

o *Skills unutilized* – underestimating the potential of people, under-utilizing them by putting them in the wrong job or holding back delegation, thus preventing them from growing in their job

Lean Strategies for Lean Processes

How do I apply these principles to procedure-development?

Here are six strategies to create effective procedures for lean processes:

1. **Remove waste.** Is the process step really necessary? Would the customer complain if the step were not being performed? If no, then the step is most likely waste and it

should be removed. The goal is to remove waste to maximize the value-add of each step.

2. **Make the work efficient.** What is the best practice? Write clear instructions describing how to perform each step. The goal is to reduce cycle-time to a minimum.

3. **Reduce interfaces.** What is the minimum number of steps? What is the most efficient sequence? Is it possible to combine several activities in one process step? Can the same person do the work? The goal here is to reduce the number of interfaces and "hand-offs" between people.

4. **Optimize ergonomics.** Is the layout optimal or can it be improved to make the work easier? Are all items and information required easily accessible? The goal is to avoid unnecessary motion.

5. **Arrange all remaining steps optimally.** Is it necessary to process all steps in series or can some steps be performed in parallel? Optimize the sequence of steps to an efficient flow. The goal is to shorten the lead-time from start to finish.

6. **Assign ownership properly.** Who is in charge? Are the right people performing the work? Who is responsible for the result?

Can some activities be delegated? The goal is to maximize the potential of people, help them build capability, grow, and take ownership. This allows decisions to be made by those people closest to the work.

Procedures

Standard Operating Procedures

In clinical research, a standard operating procedure (SOP) is defined as a "detailed, written instruction to achieve uniformity of the performance of a specific function."[1]

In business, an SOP is defined as a written instruction detailing all the steps and activities of a process. The International Organization for Standardization, or ISO (a worldwide federation of national standards), requires the documentation of all procedures that can affect the quality of a product.

A simple example of a guide or procedure in your personal life would be an instruction sheet on how to assemble a piece of furniture or use the new espresso machine. Follow the instructions correctly and you will have a correctly assembled piece of furniture and freshly brewed espresso. A more complex example would be the instruction booklet that accompanies your annual tax return

[1] International Conference on Harmonisation, ICH

33

forms. This is a much more complicated process, so it is a booklet rather than a sheet.

5 Steps to Build a Standard Operating Procedure

That is enough theory for now. Let's dive in and learn how to standardize processes and create professional work instructions. An SOP consists of five parts: Title, Code, Frame, Instruction, and History.

| 1. Title | 2 Code | 3 Frame | 4 Instruction | 5 History |

Title

The title is a meaningful header for the procedure.

Code

An alphanumerical code that allows you to classify, organize, and file the procedure.

Frame

Key parameters and procedure overview:

SIPOC = Supplier + Input + Process + Output + Customer

MOTIV = Metric + Owner + Time&Trigger + Interfaces + Validity

Instruction

This is a detailed description of what to do, how to do it, who will do it, and when.

History

This consists of the change records listed by date, change, and approver's name. These changes reflect how the procedure has evolved from its inception.

Standards

Work Standards

A work standard is an accepted reference point that allows accurate assessment of a work product. Following are the most common types of work standard:

1. **Standard Operating Procedure** – The SOP is a highly *descriptive* document with lots of text, and is ideal for standardizing administrative work processes.

2. **Standard Work Chart (SWC)** – The SWC is highly *visual*, uses many pictures, and is ideal for standardizing manual work processes.

3. **Standard Work Instruction (SWI)** – The SWI is essentially a blend between the SOP and the SWC, and has a broad range of applications.

These three work standard types use different formats but have the same role: standardizing processes and providing an accepted reference point to judge work and results.

"Standard Work" is a term coined by "Lean Practitioners," which are those who manage and optimize work standards. Standard Work is a process to specify tasks, sequence of work, cycle time, task time, and required amount of inventory.

Do I need work standards like these in my business?

To answer this question, let's utilize a tool I call the vacation test. First, imagine you go on a vacation to a remote island in the Pacific Ocean. You sleep in a hut near the beach, and this hut has no telephone or electricity. In fact, the entire island has no telephone or Internet access facilities.

Are you comfortable staying on this island, or do you feel anxious about your business and how it is operating in your absence? If you are comfortable, then you likely have adequate procedures and systems in place to handle the workload without your presence. If, however, you feel anxious, there is a high probability that you—personally—are a bottleneck in the operation of your business. This means that others depend on your work, your input, your output, and your decisions. Thus, some of the work stops when you leave, and your people are partially or entirely idle during your absence.

Why are there no formal work standards in place?

Common answers to this question are: "Nobody can do what I do," or "People make mistakes, so I have to do it," or "I'm the expert, I know what I'm doing." This simply shows that your business processes are built around *individuals* and not around *standards*.

When you build business processes around individuals, you become vulnerable and increase your risk. This is because when people move—an employee exits the workforce or goes on vacation—processes collapse and results are at risk. By simply standardizing processes and issuing formal work standards, you mitigate this risk significantly.

Where do you start?

You typically start standardizing processes in those areas for which you want better results. You can (1) analyze critical processes that are currently formalized but delivering poor results, and (2) look at those processes which haven't yet been formalized to capture new opportunities.

What are the typical concerns or objections to work standards?

Process owners express three main concerns when they are requested to standardize and delegate their work. First, many people feel that when delegation occurs there will be a loss of control. Others might fear that they need to work harder or that introducing too much standardization will result in a loss of flexibility and thus customer responsiveness.

o Delegation = loss of control
o Commitment = loss of freedom
o Standardization = loss of flexibility

These concerns are rooted in the fear of becoming replaceable. A common statement I hear is, "When everyone can do the job, why do they need me?" Other people fear they are losing choices, and they might say, "When everything is fixed, how can I apply my skill and show my capability?"

Another concern relates to accountability. When there are no methods in place for effective measurement of process performance, no one receives the blame when a failure occurs. With work standards in place, this is no longer true and people assume more responsibility for the results of their labor.

To create and implement successful work standards, such as an SOP, you must address these common concerns.

Benefits of Standardization

Peace of mind is paramount

First of all, by implementing work standards in your business, you will free up your time because you will no longer be a bottleneck. This will result in less stress.

Probably the most important thing in life is your health and well being. High stress has been correlated to health problems, high blood pressure being a prominent example. If you can formalize your processes, procedures, and standards such that you are allowed to go on vacation—without feeling anxious over your business—you will hopefully live a longer, happier life.

Efficiencies in product quality and cost

Other benefits relate more directly to product quality and cost. For example, process performance is measured in QCD metrics, which consider three parameters: (1) quality, (2) cost and (3) delivery. Traditional thinking limits most people when it comes to QCD metrics. They wrongly believe that only *two* dimensions can be improved on, and this can only be done at the expense of the third metric. For example, someone might say, "A quick and cheap meal can't be made out of the finest quality ingredients," or, "To reliably get a package delivered overnight, you have to pay a premium."

However, this common limitation in thinking does not apply to process standardization. When transforming an unstructured work process into a standardized work process, all three metrics are improved simultaneously, so the work can be done faster, more reliably, and at a lower cost.

Less variability means higher quality

"Quality is not an act, it is a habit." - Aristotle, ancient Greek philosopher, scientist and physician, 384 BC-322 BC

Procedures provide clear instructions. By specifying exactly what to do and exactly how to do it, uncertainty is removed, variability is reduced, and the work is more repeatable. The overall process is more stable, and the results are more consistent and predictable.

Higher effectiveness lowers costs

Formal procedures reduce expenses because a standardized process can be delegated to less costly employees or outsourced to external specialists. These procedures thus allow key people to focus resources on core activities.

Shorter cycles for faster delivery

Procedures are "best practices," describing the most effective way to work under given constraints. They describe all essential tasks and required quality levels. Steps that do not add value, such as double handling, trial-and-error, and frequent corrections due to unclear instructions, are removed. Process cycle times and lead-times are reduced, allowing for faster delivery and shorter time-to-market.

Faster learning for rapid implementation

"Those that know, do. Those that understand, teach." – Aristotle, ancient Greek philosopher, scientist and physician, 384 BC-322 BC

Formal procedures shorten the learning curve dramatically, making training much more effective than verbal instructions alone. Working with formal procedures typically increases process-quality by one sigma-level or more, so the results will depend more on the process and less on the individuals giving the verbal instructions or those performing the work.

Procedures enable Kaizen!

"Keep up the old standards, and day by day raise them higher." - John Wanamaker, American merchant, religious leader, and marketing pioneer, 1838–1922

Kaizen (Japanese for "improvement") is a philosophy that focuses on continuous process improvement in manufacturing, engineering, and business management. But remember, only standardized processes can be improved. You can't measure a significant performance improvement from a process if you haven't already written down how to perform the work. So, before you think about practicing Kaizen, document your process to get a stable reference point, regardless of how good or bad the current situation is. By recording today's processes as SOPs, you will stimulate thinking, trigger new ideas, and improve key dimensions by at least 20% (based on 38 SOP-introductions in 5 different industries, reducing cycle-time and rework-rate).

Reduce your carbon footprint by reducing defects

Procedures define the best way to meet customer expectations with minimal resource consumption. Without a standard, customer requirements are often unclear and people are left to use their best assumptions, which are not always correct. Lack of standards leads to waste from overproduction, overprocessing, and defects. You may be delivering more or better than what the customer requires, or spending excessive resources on (1) rectifying problems such as rework, repair, scrap, and (2) extra efforts to regain customer confidence. Those wastes increase cost, resource consumption, and therefore your carbon footprint.

You might start by asking the following questions: How often does a process run perfectly, without any stoppage or rework? How often does it not? Compare these numbers with and without a formal work standard. As a rule of thumb, introducing a work standard cuts defects and delays by 50%.

This means that if a particular process has a defect rate of 10%, and you implement a work standard to decrease it by half, to 5%, quality level (yield) increases from 90% to 95%. Under the simple assumption that defects are directly proportional to carbon emissions, the carbon footprint will thus decrease by 5 points—and this without investing in additional assets or expensive technology. This amazing result can be attained simply by writing the process down and following this "best practice"!

Barriers to Standardization

In summary, when work standards are not present, effective delegation is limited because job requirements remain unclear. There is no reliable reference point to measure performance against, and results are unpredictable since process outcomes depend on a worker's mood, skill, and assumptions rather than on a formal procedure.

Misconceptions, fear, and lack of skills are the main causes of objections to standardization. People feel they will become obsolete and unneeded; the "tribal knowledge" has been shared and thus the secret they once held is out, making them more dispensable. People also fear taking the blame for possible failures, which are more measurable with work standards in place, and they feel they have lost the flexibility to innovate.

The following table contrasts opposing arguments for and against standard procedures. This will illustrate the contrary ways of thinking about standard operating procedures.

(–) CON STANDARD PROCEDURE"	(+) PRO STANDARD PROCEDURE"
The Protection Mindset" holds you back.	The Improvement Mindset" moves you forward.
When I write a procedure, other people can do my work and I might become obsolete and lose my job.	When I write a procedure, other people can do my work, so I can grow and do more valuable work.
When everything is defined and responsibilities are assigned, I might be blamed for the outcome.	When everything is defined, then I know exactly what is expected from me and everyone else.
When the process is defined and my performance is measured, everyone can see my weaknesses when I am late or do not do my job well. I don't like that.	When the process is defined and performance measured, I get valuable feedback on what I do well and where I can further improve. I like that.
When all steps are defined, flexibility disappears, and everything is rigid and fixed.	When all steps are defined, there is clarity where I can be flexible and where I have to be strict.
While I keep the process-knowledge to myself, I remain the expert and all decisions must go through me.	When I keep the process knowledge to myself, the entire load is on my shoulders. Therefore I prefer to share, enable others to learn, take responsibility, and grow.

Continued on next page

(–) CON STANDARD PROCEDURE"	(+) PRO STANDARD PROCEDURE"
The Protection Mindset" holds you back.	**The Improvement Mindset" moves you forward.**
Using standard procedures means more bureaucracy, more papers, and less time for actual work.	Using standard procedures means more efficiency, and fewer resources are wasted on double handling and rework.
If the process is not broken, don't change it.	If the process is not broken, break it and improve it. Competition never sleeps, so do it as long as you can, before you must and can't.
Keep what works. Never change a winning team.	The only constant is change. Continuously upgrading skills, processes, and systems are the prerequisite to remaining competitive.
Standards fix the method and way we work. Standards kill all innovation.	Standards define just one method, so everyone is challenged to find a better one; they fuel innovation.

BUILDING THE STANDARD OPERATING PROCEDURE

Y ou are just five steps away from transforming chaos into order and uncontrolled actions into standardized work:

1. *Define the title* – Provide a meaningful name for the process.
2. *Assign a code to organize the procedure* – Use codes to identify the process for easy search and retrieval functions.
3. *Define the framework* – Provide a consistent reference to get a "one-minute-overview" of the entire procedure.
4. *Define the instructions* – Write detailed instructions on how to perform the work.
5. *Maintain the history* – Record the history by tracking revisions and changes in the process.

Now select a process on the micro level, any work that is repeated frequently, such as daily manning, weekly planning, or monthly reporting.

If you are just beginning to transform your processes, start with a process that is used more frequently. Doing so will provide feedback quicker, and this feedback can then be used as input to further improve the process. The "Daily Order Entry" process for example will provide feedback 220 times faster than the "Annual Budgeting" process, so it is much better suited for learning and rapid SOP-deployment.

I will present multiple examples for each section so that you gain a clear understanding of how to form these codes for procedures in your own business. These methods will allow for creation of codes that support simple searching based on various criteria.

I will also provide detailed examples in the Exercises and Examples section of this book. That section will present both business and non-business examples that are easy to follow and understand.

Step 1 – Define the Title

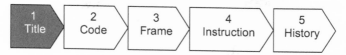

First of all, your procedure needs a title, a meaningful description of what the procedure is all about. Keep it short and to the point, like the header of a newspaper article. Ideally you want a title that is three to ten words arranged using one of the following structures:

o "How-to + verb + object" or

o "Verb-ing + object"

Here are some examples:

o "How to plan production" or
  "Planning production"
o "How to calculate commissions" or
  "Calculating commissions"
o "How to report financials" or
  "Reporting financials"
o "How to create a progress report" or
  "Creating a progress report"
o "How to prepare a conference" or
  "Preparing a conference"
o "How to assemble a cabinet" or
  "Assembling a cabinet"

o "How to replace a defective fuse" or
   "Replacing a defective fuse"
o "How to serve a guest" or
   "Serving a guest"
o "How to behave in an emergency" or
   "Behaving in an emergency"
o "How to respond to a call" or
   "Responding to a call"
o "How to hire a new employee" or
   "Hiring a new employee"
o "How to create a control chart" or
   "Creating a control chart"
o "How to evaluate quality level" or
   "Evaluating quality level"
o "How to solve a complaint" or
   "Solving a complaint"
o "How to develop a new product" or
   "Developing a new product"
o "How to qualify a new vendor" or
   "Qualifying a new vendor"

Choose your preference of the two forms—using "How to…" or "…ing"—and keep that structure as the standard for naming procedures.

Step 2 – Assign a Code

Information is as valuable as it is applicable, understandable, and accessible. Using a logical code helps to classify and organize information, so a specific Standard Operating Procedure can be found within seconds of clicking (on a computer) or searching (for paper).

The preferred way to organize information into codes varies between individuals and organizations; therefore, I will introduce just one simple and proven method that has been successfully applied in the manufacturing industry.

Core Processes

Core processes build the value-chain, covering technical (PLM), supply (SCM), commercial (CRM), and manufacturing (MFG) processes:

- o PLM – Product Lifecycle Management – engineering processes covering all technical aspects from research to phase-out
- o SCM – Supply Chain Management – purchasing, sourcing, warehousing, and logistics processes

- o CRM – Customer Relationship Management – commercial processes, including marketing, sales, and customer service
- o MFG – Manufacturing – conversion from raw materials to finished goods or service delivery for non-manufacturing

Support Processes

Support processes enable the value chain, covering quality, personnel, finance, and data processes:

- o QM – Quality Management – quality appraisal, continuous improvement, Lean Sigma, and operations excellence processes
- o FC – Finance and Controlling – financial, accounting, and controlling processes
- o HR – Human Resources – personnel processes, employee hiring, development, and retention
- o IT – Information Technology – data collection, storage, access, security, analysis, and reporting

Code Components

The code for the procedure is built out of three components = [Process] + [Counter] + [Date]:

- o Process – use codes for core-processes (PLM, SCM, CRM, MFG) and support processes (QM, FC, HR, IT) o Counter – assign a free running number to each process – a 3-digit number allows addressing 999 procedures per process

o Date – assign a six-digit date-code to indicate the publish date, use YYMMDD-format (year-month-day) for auto-sorting

Procedure Code

When you construct the final code for the procedure, it will include the prefix [SOP]+ [Process] + [Counter] + [Date].

Here are some examples of procedure codes:

o SOP_PLM_123_150306

This example refers to an engineering procedure #123 from 2015.03.06, which translates to March 6th in the year 2015.

o SOP_CRM_726_141202

This would be the code for a commercial procedure #726 from 2014.12.02 (December, 2, 2014).

o SOP_FC_009_120930

This code refers to a finance procedure #009 from September 30, 2012.

o SOP_QM_522_160401

This code if for a quality procedure #522 from April 1st, 2016.

Notice how we can easily form search strings once these procedures are input into a database. For example, to find and return all the finance procedures, we could form a database query that searches these procedure codes for the string "*_FC_*". The database entries coded for finance would be returned by the system.

We could also form search strings that selected entries with various dates. For example, we could select out all procedures coded with a date from a particular year and month.

Procedure File Name

Procedures should be saved in a search-friendly format, so they can be found and retrieved in 10 seconds or less. As search methods vary between companies and systems, we apply the simplest form of indexing—using the file name as reference.

Here some examples from manufacturing and administration:

- o SOP_PLM_123_150306_changing_engineering_drawing
- o SOP_CRM_726_141202_forecasting_quarterly_demand
- o SOP_FC_009_120930_reporting_monthly_financials
- o SOP_QM_522_160401_inbound_quality_check

Step 3 – Define the Framework

The framework gives readers a quick overview of what the procedure is all about. It lists all key parameters, such as input and output, supplier and customer, time and trigger, etc. Regardless of scope, length, or type of the procedure, the framework is a consistent reference to get a "one-minute-overview" of the entire procedure.

For an effective procedure framework, we can apply the SIPOC-model from the Six Sigma world:

SIPOC – Process Parameters

- o Supplier – delivers resources, such as items and information
- o Input – items and information required for the process
- o Process – main steps to convert input into output
- o Output – outcome or deliverable of the process
- o Customer – beneficiary of the process output

The SIPOC model covers technical process parameters, such as resources, inputs, outputs, etc. To write effective procedures however, we also need to consider the managerial dimension as well and add five control parameters to our existing SIPOC-model + MOTIV.

MOTIV – Control Parameters

- o Metric – a performance indicator to measure effectiveness
- o Owner – the person responsible for process and procedure
- o Time Trigger – process trigger and process duration
- o Include – other procedures and references to be considered
- o Validity – scope of the process, regional or functional validity

Putting both together, SIPOC+MOTIV gives readers a quick and effective overview of all process parameters. Now let's go through this step-by-step:

SIPOC/S – Supplier

Suppliers deliver the Inputs. The easiest way to identify Suppliers is by defining the Inputs first, and then to define who provides them.

Here are some examples for Suppliers:

- o Investors (provide funding)

o Vice Presidents (provide targets)
o External Vendors (provide parts, supplies, services)
o Coaches (provide knowledge, feedback, orientation)
o Sales Representative (provide requirements, forecasts)

SIPOC/I – Input

Inputs are resources required by the process, such as parts, funding, and information.

Here are some examples for Inputs. These are analog to the ones listed for Suppliers:

o Funding (supplied by Investors)
o Targets (supplied by Vice Presidents)
o Parts (supplied by external Vendors)
o Knowledge (supplied by Coaches)
o Forecasts (supplied by Sales Representatives)

SIPOC/P – Process

For "Process," identify the three to five key steps without going into details.

Here are some examples for key steps:

o Specify–Order–Receive

(sourcing process)
- o Define–Design–Validate
  (design process)
- o Plan–Do–Check–Act
  (PDCA management process)
- o Define–Measure–Analyze–Improve–Control
  (Six Sigma process)
- o Research–Design–Validate–Release
  (engineering process)

SIPOC/O – Output

For "Output," identify the desired results. Such deliverables are specified *qualitatively*, as in "meets target" or *quantitatively*, as in "Increase by 20%."

Here are some examples:

- o Funds are available for investment
- o Quality at or above target level
- o Production plan released
- o Customer complaints solved within 5 days
- o Backlog below 5% of sales
- o Finished goods inventory below 2 weeks
- o Orders filled within 30 minutes
- o Investment request approved
- o Market share gain of 10% per year

SIPOC/C – Customer

For "Customer," identify the recipient and beneficiary of the output. A customer can be internal and external. In most cases, there are demands from both, the Voice of the Customer VOC and the Voice of the Business VOB to be satisfied.

- o External Customer – the external customer who will receive the goods or services. In most cases, the external customer is a retailer, distributor, or end-consumer of the product or service.

- o Internal Customer – the process using the output of the previous process as input. The finance department might be the internal customer of the logistics department, which delivers the daily shipping report to the controllers.

The above identify the SIPOC elements. Now let's address the MOTIV components.

MOTIV/M – Metric

For "Metric," identify how process performance is measured. Remember: without measurement, there is no management. The most basic metrics are Quality and Quantity.

Here are some examples, and they are self-explanatory:

- o Time from order to cash
- o Time from idea to launch
- o First pass yield
- o Market share growth
- o Return on assets
- o Customer satisfaction
- o Design success rate
- o Deviation from budget
- o Sales per employee
- o End-to-end margin
- o Cycle time reduction

MOTIV/O – Owner

The "Owner" is the person responsible for the procedure, defining the standard, how to work. The procedure owner has the following responsibilities:

- o Identify the best way to work (together with people performing the work)
- o Develop the Standard Operating Procedure
- o Implement the procedure and train people on the new standard
- o Set targets and measure performance
- o Collect feedback and continuously improve process and procedure

MOTIV/T – Time & Trigger

The "Time" defines the maximum cycle-time, or duration, of the process. The "Trigger" defines how the process is being started. The following are some key considerations:

o Time-trigger – like a TRAIN, the process runs regularly, at a fixed time, daily, weekly, monthly, quarterly, or annually, according to a specific schedule.

o Event-trigger – like a TAXI, the process starts when triggered by a phone call, entry, demand, confirmation, alarm, request, etc.

o Cycle-time – the maximum acceptable duration is called process cycle time. It defines the "Time-out," which specifies when the process must be completed.

MOTIV/I – Interfaces

The "Interfaces" are the connections between processes. They specify the link between this SOP and other policies, procedures, manuals, references, or regulations.

Here are some Interface examples:

o See HR-Manual for more information on behavioral standard 'Code of Conduct'

o See SOP-0292A "Machine Setup" for detailed setup instructions

o See SOP-1237B "Return Goods to Vendor" to return failed items to vendor
o See local labor laws when scheduling overtime on weekends and holidays
o See original customer specification sheet to validate test data

MOTIV/V – Validity

The "Validity" defines the function, region, model, or condition the procedure is valid for.

Here are some examples:

o Global purchasing procedure (valid worldwide, all purchasing)
o APAC hiring procedure (valid only for the region Asia Pacific)
o E-class manual (valid only for a specific product or model)
o EUR currency transactions (valid only for Euro currency)

Step 4 – Define the Instructions

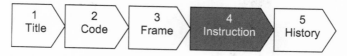

The next step is to define the instructions, where the "Instruction" is the heart of the procedure. This guides the users step-by-step through the process. The structure is very simple; it consists of the following three elements (think 3W) for each task:

o WHAT needs to be done and how to do it
o WHO is responsible for performing the task
o WHEN the task is to be completed

3W/WHAT

The "What" describes the task that needs to be completed and the way to accomplish it. A very effective way to specify tasks is "military style". Such top-down order is straightforward and ensures the utmost clarity. Task description should (1) be short, (2) start with a verb followed by a noun, and (3) contain 3 to 10 words maximum. The entire task-description should fit into a single row of text. The shorter it is, the more focused and clearer the instruction will be. The description (what to do) follows the task-details (how to do it), guiding users through all details. After each task description, specify the desired outcome. Defining the "Result" helps the user judge if the work was done correctly.

Example - How to Prepare Coffee

1. Ask guest how many cups they like
2. Pour water into coffee maker, 0.2l/cup
3. Scoop coffee powder, 1 scoop/cup
4. Switch-on, brew coffee, 1 min/cup
5. Pour coffee into cups
6. Add sugar and creamer on side
7. Result: coffee served within 5 min

3W/WHO

The "Who" describes the person responsible, also known as the task-owner.

Here are some guidelines on how to assign tasks to owners:

o   Single owner per task – to avoid ambiguity, only one person can be in charge for each task.

o   If several people are involved, split task into smaller tasks so that the first rule is met— one owner per task.

o   For task-owners, use titles, NOT names— so the procedure remains valid even when there are people or organizational changes.

o If a team needs to deliver something, the group leader is assigned as task-owner, and this person is responsible for the entire group.

3W/WHEN

The "When" describes the timing, which specifies when the task must be completed "time-out." The timing can be specified *relative* or *absolute*.

Here are some examples:

o Every Friday before 5pm (a time reference)
o At the 3rd work-day of each month (a time reference)
o One day after receiving an order (an event reference)
o Immediate when the alarm light flashes (an event reference)
o When arriving at the office (an event reference)

Steps and Numbering

Each process step contains one or several tasks. The same person, the task owner, performs all of the steps. Assign a sequential number to each step as a reference. Example: "Step seven needs to be completed one week after step six."

Here are some rules for process steps and numbering:

- o Each step can only have one owner.
- o A number is assigned to each step.
- o Each step lists tasks that are to be completed by the same owner in series.

Step 5 – Maintain the History

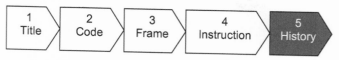

A procedure is based on assumptions that are made at a specific point in time. While conditions, assumptions, and requirements continuously change, processes and procedures need to evolve and adapt. All changes affecting fit, form, or function are considered "major changes" and must be formally controlled. To ensure full traceability, record the actual change, the approver's name, and the release date in the SOP revision history log:

- o *Date* –when update was released
- o *Update* – what exactly was changed
- o *Approval* – who approved the change

Here is an example of Procedure History:

- o 2014.03.20 Initial procedure design, released by Robert G.
- o 2014.05.03 Added validation step #7, approved by Andrea V.
- o 2014.06.03 Step #18 from 2 days to 1 day, approved by David S.

EXERCISES AND EXAMPLES

*L*et's apply what we have learned so far in the following exercise:

Translate this BOOK into an SOP.

The task is to write a procedure that explains how to write procedures. The outcome is an SOP about writing SOPs, and this is an excellent way to check your understanding.

Here are the details of this procedure:

- o The title of this SOP would be "Creating Standard Operating Procedures"
- o The Human Resource department would lead the SOP development
- o This is 37th HR-procedure created, so the number would be "HR_37"

o The publish date of this procedure is 01-June-2015, so the date code would be: 2015.06.01

o Therefore, the file name would be:

"SOP_HR_037_150601_Creating_Standard_ Operating_Procedures"

There are many different ways to solve this exercise. All procedures created will be different, dependent on the assumptions, skills, and experiences of the creator. Do NOT read on before completing this exercise. Then compare your solution with the one I offer (right after the template). What did you do differently?

The purpose of comparing the different procedures is to identify the most effective way to get to the destination, the "Best Practice SOP."

SOP Exercise Template

Now it's time to fill the template. Write the instruction on how to create standard procedures. Be specific. Be clear. Do it now.

CODE + TITLE

FRAME	
Supplier	
Input	
Process	
Output	
Customer	
Metric	
Owner	
Time/Trigger	
Interfaces	
Validity	

INSTRUCTION			
#	What + How	Who	When
0			
1			
2			

HISTORY		
Date	Revision	Approval

You can download this SOP and other tools and templates at: www.leanmap.com/support

SOP Exercise Solution

Here is one possible solution for the procedure on creating procedures. Remember, there is no right or wrong way to do this, just differences in efficiency and effectiveness.

CODE+TITLE
SOP_HR_037_150601Creating Standard Operating Procedures

FRAME	
Supplier	Operators, manager
Input	Observations, flow charts
Process	Identify best way > write procedure > test and optimize > approve and release
Output	Standard Operating Procedure (SOP)
Customer	Operators performing the work
Metric	Percentage of process operations completed without any defect or delay
Owner	Assigned process owner per organizational chart
Time/Trigger	Time to create an SOP is 3 days, triggered when process results are unreliable
Interfaces	Consider existing documentation rules, such as ISO, when creating SOPs

FRAME	
Validity	This procedure is valid for all functions in manufacturing and office

INSTRUCTION			
#	**What**	**Who**	**When**
0	**Initial Setup** • Implement a system to measure process performance • Set a target and limit for process variability • Result: process management system is set up	Process Owner (Manger)	Initial Setup
1	**Identify a Problem** • Measure and record process results • If variability exceeds limit, alert the process owner • Result: process owner is informed about the problem	Operator	Anytime
2	**Determine the Cause** • Identify the cause for the process variation • If cause is unstructured work, call team to create SOP • Result: team meeting setup to identify best way to work	Process Owner (Manager)	3 days max after alert (step-1)

INSTRUCTION			
#	**What**	**Who**	**When**
3	**Identify the Best Practice** • Hold team meeting with key operators and supervisors • Walk the process to see how work is actually performed • Use process analysis tools to determine best way (VSM etc) • Draft the Standard Operating Procedure • Result: SOP is defined and ready for test	QA Manager guides the meeting	1 week after alert (step-1)
4	**Introduce New Procedure** • Teach people on the standard process and procedure • Write a test-plan to test SOP under different conditions • Result: operators are ready to test new SOP	Process Owner (Manager)	2 weeks after alert (step-1)
5	**Test New Procedure** • Work exactly according to new procedure • Measure process quality, quantity, and timing • Record of problems and improvement ideas • Result: process performance if formally recorded	Supervisor	2 weeks for testing

INSTRUCTION			
#	What	Who	When
6	**Approval and Release** • Optimize procedure based on data and feedback • Approve and publish final SOP • Archive in central system and display at point-of-use • Result: SOP is controlled and accessible	Process Owner	1 month after alert

HISTORY		
Date	Revision	Approval
2015.05.01	Request to standardize process due to 30% delays recorded	Henry C.
2015.05.08	Process mapped and first SOP draft version released for test	Mary K.
2015.06.01	Process optimized and final procedure (SOP) released	Andreas K.

You can download this SOP and other tools and templates at: www.leanmap.com/support

SOP Administration Example – Solving Complaints

A very common procedure in business administration is solving quality problems, such as customer complaints. For the following example, let's assume that Quality Management (QM) has the lead on this procedure and it is the 122nd procedure created in the QM department, and it was issued on the 17-April-2016.

CODE+TITLE
SOP_QM_122_160417 Solving Quality Problems

FRAME	
Supplier	Anyone who identified a problem (internal or external customer)
Input	Quality case (problem formally recorded)
Process	Identify > solve > prevent (using 8D problem solving method)
Output	Solution implemented and root-cause eliminated
Customer	Internal or external customer (anyone impacted by the problem)
Metric	Number of problems recorded, percentage of cases solved within 30 days
Owner	Quality Assurance (QA), head of department
Time/Trigger	Process starts when problem was recorded, 30 days to solve and close case
Interfaces	HR handbook, customer call procedure 2345, cost accounting guideline 1134B
Validity	Global process, valid for all entities

INSTRUCTION			
#	**What**	**Who**	**When**
0	**Record Problem** • External customers call service center to record problem • Internal customers enter problem directly in Q-system • Result: problem is formally recorded	Anyone	During office hours
1	**Minor Problem Solving** • For minor problem, solve per customer service handbook • For major problems (not in handbook), escalate to level-2 • Result: problem solved at level-1 or escalated to level-2	Customer Service Member	During call Anytime
2	**Major Problem Routing** • Major problems are addressed by team leader • If team-leader cannot solve, escalate to level-3 (Quality) • Result: problem solved at level-2 or escalated to level-3	Customer Service Leader	1hr. after call
3	**Assemble Team (D1)** • Quality department was notified of the new Q-case • Select people required to address the complaint • Assign roles and responsibilities of all team members • Result: team and team-leader is assigned, step D1 done	Head of Quality	2hr. after call

	INSTRUCTION		
#	**What**	**Who**	**When**
4	**Identify Problem (D2)** • Get facts, symptoms, and background information • Describe the problem as precise as you can • Result: problem statement properly defined, step D2 done	Assigned Q-Case Leader	4hr. after call
5	**Contain Problem (D3)** • Develop a containment measure "quick fix" to prevent the problem from spreading (band-aid to stop the bleeding) • Inform customer of containment measure • Result: problem is contained, step D3 done	Assigned Q-Case Leader	3 days after call
6	**Analyze Cause (D4)** • Perform full root-cause analysis • Use Fishbone diagram, fault-tree analysis, 5-whys • Get sufficient data for confidence factor above 90% • Result: root-cause determined, step D4 done	Assigned Q-Case Leader	7 days after call

INSTRUCTION			
#	**What**	**Who**	**When**
7	**Develop Solution (D5)** • Determine the permanent solution • Be aware of the difference between SOLUTION and FIX • FIX addresses the SYMPTIONS (= temporary success) • SOLUTION addresses the CAUSES (= permanent success) • Result: solution is proven to remove cause, step D5 done	Assigned Q-Case Leader	14 days after call
8	**Implement Solution (D6)** • Develop implementation plan and enter in PJM system • Lead the implementation, manage the critical chain • Keep all stakeholders informed (especially the customer) • Result: solution is fully implemented, step D6 done	Assigned Q-Case Leader	21 days after call

INSTRUCTION			
#	**What**	**Who**	**When**
9	**Prevent Problem (D7)** • Avoid re-occurrence by error-proofing process and system • Consider "Poka-Yoke" techniques where appropriate • Improve process and system, update SOPs • Measure effectiveness of error-proof process, collect data • Result: problem cannot repeat, step D7 done	Assigned Q-Case Leader	28 days after call
10	**Close Case (D8)** • Conclude the case and communicate results • Inform everyone on new procedures and system updates • Release team and thank everyone for their contribution • Result: case is closed, step D8 done	Assigned Q-Case Leader	30 days after call
11	**Monthly Business Review (MBR)** • Report number of Q-cases (open, solved, days in process) • Determine impact on customer and financials • Report severity, trend, and non-performance cost (NPC) • Result: executive team is informed	Head of Quality	Every first Friday of the month

HISTORY		
Date	**Revision**	**Approval**
2016.03.20	First SOP-draft by teams from Quality and Customer Service	L. Harrison
2016.04.17	Draft SOP updated with step-11, approved, and released	H. Anders

You can download this SOP and other tools and templates at: www.leanmap.com/support

SOP Warehouse Example – Cycle Counting

The following procedure describes the process of cycle counting inventory with the intent of keeping stock quantities accurate in the Material Resource Planning (MRP) system. In this example, we assume that Supply Chain Management (SCM) is in charge of the procedure. It's the 68th procedure created in the SCM department, and the issue date for this procedure will be 22-August-2016.

CODE+TITLE
SOP_SCM_068_160822Cycle Counting Inventory

FRAME	
Supplier	Head of supply chain management (SCM)
Input	ABC-Analysis to determine items (SKU's) to be counted

FRAME	
Process	Decide items to be counted > count > update system
Output	Stock quantity in systems is accurate
Customer	Production planner
Metric	Deviation between system and counted quantity (%items with deviation)
Owner	Warehouse team leader
Time/Trigger	Every week for 3 hours per counting session
Interfaces	Inventory report, delivery performance report, stock-out report
Validity	Local XYZ factory warehouse only

INSTRUCTION			
#	What	Who	When
0	**Initial Setup** • Define criteria for ABC-items (A=custom … C=commodity) • Review master data and assign ABC-code to all items • Result: all items in system have ABC-code assigned	Head of Home	Initial Setup
1	**Prepare for Cycle Count** • Log into planning system (MRP) and print ABC-report • Assign team members to carry-out the cycle count • Result: team equipped and ready for cycle count	Warehouse Manager	Thursdays before 8am Anytime

INSTRUCTION			
#	What	Who	When
2	**Cycle Count** • Go to warehouse location and perform cycle count • Write quantity on ABC-report behind each item • Return report to warehouse manager • Result: cycle count completed	Team Member	Thursdays before 11am
3	**Update System** • Enter the counted quantity in the system • For deviation over 0.1%, create a RCA fishbone analysis • Issue corrective action for planning and logistics process • Enter count accuracy in warehouse control chart • Result: >99.9% accurate stock or <1/1000 SKU-deviation	Warehouse Manager	Thursdays before 5pm

HISTORY		
Date	Revision	Approval
2016.08.10	Stock cycle count process defined and procedure drafted	Douglas B.

HISTORY		
Date	**Revision**	**Approval**
2016.08.21	Improvement implemented, root-cause analysis/fishbone added	Jose F.
2016.08.22	Improvement approved and revised procedure released	Maria G.

You can download this SOP and other tools and templates at: www.leanmap.com/support

SOP Parenting Example – Keeping Family Life

Procedures are not only applicable to the business environment; they can also be used in your personal and professional life. Everyone with kids knows how challenging it can be to keep rooms clean, the kitchen organized, bedtimes on schedule, TV time within limits, and school grades on target. The following example shows how the concepts in this book can be applied to family life by setting clear expectations, guidance, rewards, and consequences. The process owner in this case is the head of the family.

CODE+TITLE
SOP_HeadHome_001_151030 Keeping the Family Life

FRAME	
Supplier	Parents
Input	Rules and Expectations
Process	Set Expectations > measure progress > reward and correct > meet expectations
Output	Behavior and results on track
Customer	Parents and Kids
Metric	School-grades, pocket-money paid out, number of perfect days per month
Owner	Head of family (can be father or mother or other family member in charge)
Time/Trigger	Validated daily
Interfaces	School calendar to be considered
Validity	Valid at home

INSTRUCTION			
#	What	Who	When
0	**Initial Setup** • Involve all family members when writing this procedure • Get feedback to ensure that everyone is clear about rules • Post this procedure at a place where everyone can see it • Result: rules and process are understood	Head of Home	Initial Setup

INSTRUCTION			
#	**What**	**Who**	**When**
1	**Organize Rooms** • Put clean cloths into cabinet, dirty cloths into laundry basket • Items are on the desk or in boxes; nothing lays on the floor • Bed is made-up; see the "Good Room" picture for reference • Result: rooms are kept clean and tidy	Kids	Daily
2	**Personal Hygiene** • Brush teeth after each meal for 2 minutes minimum • Wash hands with soap after toilet and arriving at home • Take a shower every day and after sports activity • Result: basic conditions for good health maintained	Everyone	Daily

INSTRUCTION			
#	**What**	**Who**	**When**
3	**Times for Bed / Entertainment** • Weekdays: go to bed at 8:30pm, lights and music off by 9pm • Weekends: go to bed and lights off at 10:00 • Exceptions: only for major events like New Year celebration • TV/Games: 1 hours per weekday and 2 hours per weekend-day • Result: times are kept within 5 minutes tolerance per day	Kids	Daily
4	**Get Good Grades** • Get 5 points for A-grade, 2 points for B, and 0 points for C • Add the points of the last 3 exams (rolling grade system): • 12…15 points allows maximum freedom • 10…14 points means 2 days per week reserved for study • 6…9 points means 4 days per week reserved for study • 0…5 points means full-time study until grades on target • Result: average grade is at A - or better	Kids	Last 3 Exams

INSTRUCTION			
#	**What**	**Who**	**When**
5	**Ensure Food Supply** • Major shopping to buy groceries and consumables • Buy fresh items during the week, as needed • Result: refrigerator is filled, sufficient food for 7-10 days	Parents	Saturdays
6	**Maintain Household** • Clean table and load dishwasher (everyone) • Unload dishwasher when run is completed (kids) • Feed dog (Mum) • Walk dog (Kids in morning, Mum in afternoon, Dad in evening) • Vacuum carpet and mop the hard floor (Mum) • Exchange towels when dirty or older than one week (Mum) • Result: daily household work is done without arguments	All Family Members	Daily

INSTRUCTION			
#	What	Who	When
7	**Maintain Car** • Fill gas when indicator light is on • Check basics: oil, tires, wipers, fluids, break-pads (weekly) • Wash car outside with shampoo (weekly) • Clean car inside with leather and plastic cleaner (monthly) • Keep maintenance schedule (check monthly) • Deep-clean and wax application (quarterly) • Result: car is well maintained	Dad	Weekly – Monthly
8	**Monthly Budget / Bill Payment** • $xxx for groceries and household (Mum, as needed) • $xxx for rent and utility (Dad, monthly) • $xxx for major expenses, furniture, TV, vacation (parents) • $xxx for education and kids pocket money • $xxx transferred to investment account • Result: spending according budget account never overdrawn	Parents	Max 5 days after Bill arrives

INSTRUCTION			
#	What	Who	When
9	**Kids Consequences** • Minor deviation = when a rule is not exactly kept =20% reduction of monthly allowance and TV-hours. • Major deviation = when a rule was purposely broken = zero allowance and TV-hours cancelled for next month • Good grades and good behavior = 200% allowance • Result: good behavior and good results are rewarded	Kids decide, Parents give	Always
10	**Continuous Improvement** • If you find a better way to achieve the same result, mark-up this procedure and discuss in the weekly family gathering	Everyone	Sundays

HISTORY		
Date	Revision	Approval
2015.10.20	Head of family calls everyone to define rules	Mum
2015.10.22	First draft version to test the new procedure	Mum+Dad
2015.10.21	Request to change TV-hours from 30 minutes to 1hr per day	Son Mark

HISTORY		
Date	Revision	Approval
2015.10.29	Final procedure released with updated TV-hours	Mum+Dad

You can download this SOP and other tools and templates at: www.leanmap.com/support

FREQUENTLY ASKED QUESTIONS

Do procedures need formal approval?

Yes. Procedures are clear instructions how to work; they must be approved by the person responsible for the process results, typically the functional manager or supervisor.

Can a procedure cover all possible options and still be effective?

No. To cover all possible options, a procedure would become bloated and ineffective. A good compromise is achieved when the procedure covers at least 80% of the process options and variations. Apply the Pareto principle (80/20 rule) to decide which options to include.

Does each step have a result specified?

Yes. Each task has a desired outcome (deliverable) specified, such as an item, a decision, a report.

Specifying the result allows each task to be validated simply by asking: "Was the result achieved or not?"

How many details should an SOP include? Do I need to specify every little detail?

No. You should just define enough details for users to clearly understand how to perform the work. The operator with the lowest skill level is your reference to judge the degree of details required in the procedure.

Is an efficient procedure always effective?

No. Example: a report that is created rapidly and efficiently is still ineffective when not used for decision-making. "Effective" means doing the right thing, setting the right targets, generating value to the customer. "Efficient" means doing the work with minimal resources, in the fastest possible way.

Can the procedure handle exceptions?

Yes. Besides describing the standard process, the procedure can also describe exceptions, or the "escapes" from the standard. Example: You will get an answer via e-mail within one day (this is the standard). If you haven't received an answer within three days, call the vice president directly (the escape) to get an immediate answer.

Is it true that fewer standards mean more flexibility?

No. A standard does not affect flexibility at all, as what you can do and not do remains exactly the same with or without a standard. But standards guide people to the right path, eliminating poor choices and therefore making their actions and choices much more effective.

Flow charts already describe processes. Isn't that enough?

No. Flow charts just describe the flow but lack the information about how to work, who is responsible, when to start, when to complete, nor do they include metrics and escalation paths.

Which is the best format?

There is no single best format. It is a matter of preference. A text editor such as Microsoft Word is ideal for writing Standard Operating Procedures, where tables provide a clear structure while maintaining flexibility for variable text lengths. Microsoft Powerpoint is a good choice for creating Standard Work Charts since they contain more images and less text than a typical SOP. Microsoft Excel is less functional since it is more rigid and limited in number of characters per cell.

Does it make sense to split a very long process into several sub-processes?

Yes. Several shorter sub-processes are easier to manage than one comprehensive master-process.

Do all processes need to be measured consistently?

No. Measurement only makes sense to validate performance of critical processes and to drive improvement actions. Measuring stable and non-critical processes is not value adding, unnecessary bureaucracy, and pure waste.

Does it make sense to assign process ownership to everyone, making everyone responsible?

No. If everyone is assigned ownership, nobody will feel responsible and nobody will take charge and *own* the process and result. Always assign ownership for each task, process, and result.

Which processes must be standardized? Every single one?

No. Not all, but at least standardize mission-critical processes to minimize risk.

What does mission-critical mean?

Processes that harm the business if they don't work properly. For this reason, mission-critical processes are the top priorities for standardization.

The SOP-template lists tasks in series. Can it also handle parallel task processing?

Yes. Each task has its specific trigger and completion point. If, for example, task five and six run in parallel, they both refer to the same trigger-point; they start at the same time and run in parallel, even though they are listed in sequence in the table.

If a procedure is not fully defined, should I wait until it's perfected?

No. The procedure will never be perfect and you can't see all the issues unless you have tested it. To test it, you need to release it. Keep in mind that an imperfect procedure is much better than having no standard at all. Working without a procedure means 0% defined, leaving 100% chance for mistakes. Even the worst procedure is better than no procedure, as people can review, challenge and continuously improve it, perfecting the procedure over time.

When I finished writing the procedure, does it mean I can "set it and forget it?"

No. Whenever process performance is below expectations or when someone finds a better way, it's time to revise the procedure. I do this on average 10 to 15 times during the first year after a new procedure is released.

The process works well, do I really need to write a procedure for it?

No. When quality is built into the process itself, there is no need for additional bureaucracy. Only when good results are not automatic is a procedure required.

Is it OK to store the SOP on my computer?

No. Procedures are formal documents that need to be stored in a controlled document depository. This can be a central archive, database, or cloud. It is important that the procedure be easily accessible at the point of use.

How often should I update an SOP?

As a rule of thumb, at least once per year. Fast moving industries require frequent process improvements just to remain competitive; SOP updates every three to six months are common.

Does it make sense to include visuals?

Yes, absolutely. Use pictures, drawings, and screenshots where appropriate. Insert visuals below the text to improve effectiveness of the task description.

Start now!

"Go as far as you can see; when you get there, you'll be able to see farther." - John Pierpont Morgan, American financier, banker and art collector, 1837–1913

ABOUT THE AUTHOR

Joerg Muenzing is an expert in industrialization, rationalization, and business turnaround management. He is the founder and president of Leanmap, an operations consultancy firm devoted to making the world more efficient. He holds a Master's degree in business and a Bachelor's degree in engineering. He is certified black belt six sigma in auditing and lean production systems. He has managed global plant networks and designed and implemented 22 transformation programs in 14 countries for large manufacturers. He speaks on the topics of accelerating innovation, lean transformation, and cost reduction.

He has consulted with over 50 executive teams to bring their operations performance to a world-class level. Clients include Mercedes Benz, Franke, Landis & Gyr, Detroit Diesel, Navico, Techtronic Industries, Gategourmet. He lives with his family in Switzerland.

Contact information:

contact@leanmap.com

About Leanmap

Leanmap is an international operations consultancy, specializing in industrialization, rationalization and business turnarounds. We provide the strategies, world-class solutions, and interim management assistance to solve operational constraints, raise performance levels, and prepare our clients for the future. We operate from hubs in Switzerland, Hong Kong, and the United States to support a diverse, worldwide client base. We optimize operational footprints, design and implement new factory layouts, streamline processes, lead transformation programs, and bring mission-critical projects back on track. We thrive on change and enjoy solving problems while leading people to discover new ways of thinking and working.

The Leanmap Way

Our proven process of "Navigating to Results" sets us apart from traditional consulting firms simply because we *simultaneously* address people, processes, and systems to ensure that results are not only discussed but actually achieved and measured. We act as *partners* to our clients, providing end-to-end services that span the entire spectrum —from the initial diagnostics to the full implementation of a transformation or turnaround program.

We lay out new factories and develop lean processes that shorten lead and response-times, thus increasing customer satisfaction levels; we streamline research and development to get new products to market faster; we design and implement shared service centers to centralize support functions; we raise quality levels to reduce warranty exposure; and we boost operational efficiency to lower the cost base.

With our deep technical knowledge, proven management expertise, and cross-cultural skills, we lead businesses to a new level of operating performance. We do this by emphasizing cooperation. We "roll up our sleeves" and work side-by-side with our clients' teams, leading them through the entire change process until results are achieved, gains are validated, and systems are in place to sustain them.

We measure our success strictly by impact. *Hard Results* are identified as improvements in speed, quality and profitability—and they are measured by tracking key performance indicators on the balanced scorecard. *Soft Results* are identified as improvements in motivation, mindset and behavior, and are assessed by survey.

Coach, Consultant, Implementer

We offer three engagement options to meet our clients' needs. For basic engagements, we work as *coaches*, transferring knowledge to build skills and capability. If more assistance is required, we work as *consultants* to develop detailed solutions, ready for implementation. For maximum control over processes and results, we work as *interim managers* to implement solutions until results are achieved and systems are in place to sustain them.

You can count on Leanmap to transform your operation in a positive direction. For a complimentary quote, contact us at:

contact@leanmap.com

www.leanmap.com

From Chaos to Control

Made in the USA
Lexington, KY
09 January 2014